TREASURY OF NURSERY RHYMES

TREASURY OF
NURSERY RHYMES

Selected by
Alistair Hedley

Illustrated by
**Kate Aldous, Claire Henley,
Anna Cynthia Leplar, Karen Perrins, Scott Rhodes,
Jane Tattersfield and Sara Walker**

This is a Parragon Book
This edition published in 2002

Parragon
Queen Street House
4 Queen Street
Bath BA1 1HE, UK

Created by
The Albion Press Ltd

ISBN 0-75259-205-X

Printed and bound in Dubai

CONTENTS

LITTLE BOY BLUE and other rhymes of childhood   71

BAA, BAA, BLACK SHEEP and other animal rhymes   101

THE HOUSE THAT JACK BUILT and other story rhymes   131

THERE WAS AN OLD WOMAN WHO LIVED IN A SHOE
and other rhymes about grown-ups   161

ROUND AND ROUND THE GARDEN
and other action rhymes, tongue-twisters, and riddles   191

HUSH-A-BYE BABY and other bedtime rhymes   221

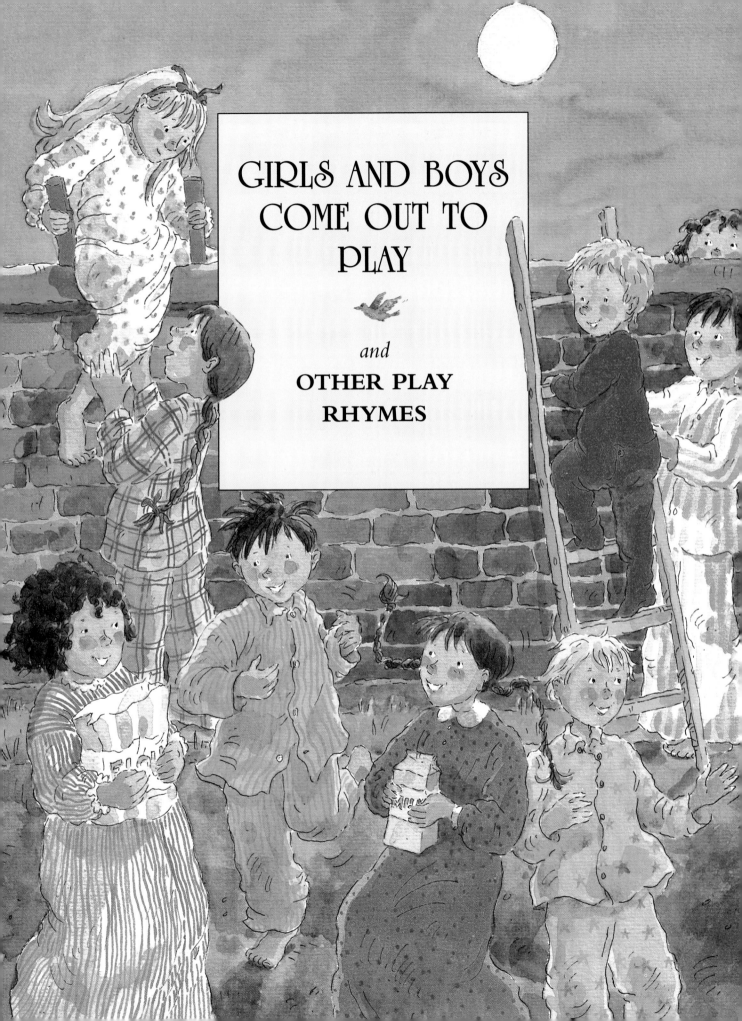

GIRLS AND BOYS COME OUT TO PLAY

and

OTHER PLAY RHYMES

GIRLS AND BOYS COME OUT TO PLAY

Girls and boys, come out to play;
The moon doth shine as bright as day;
Leave your supper, and leave your sleep,
And come with your playfellows into the street.
Come with a whoop, come with a call,
Come with a good will or not at all.
Up the ladder and down the wall,
A halfpenny roll will serve us all.
You find milk, and I'll find flour,
And we'll have a pudding in half-an-hour.

GEORGIE, PORGIE

Georgie, Porgie, pudding and pie,
Kissed the girls and made them cry;
When the boys came out to play
Georgie Porgie ran away.

I SCREAM

I scream, you scream,
We all scream for ice cream!

HERE WE GO ROUND
THE MULBERRY BUSH

Here we go round the mulberry bush,
The mulberry bush, the mulberry bush,
Here we go round the mulberry bush,
On a cold and frosty morning.

This is the way we wash our hands,
Wash our hands, wash our hands,
This is the way we wash our hands,
On a cold and frosty morning.

Here we go round the mulberry bush,
The mulberry bush, the mulberry bush,
Here we go round the mulberry bush,
On a cold and frosty morning.

This is the way we wash our clothes,
Wash our clothes, wash our clothes,
This is the way we wash our clothes,
On a cold and frosty morning.

Here we go round the mulberry bush,
The mulberry bush, the mulberry bush,
Here we go round the mulberry bush,
On a cold and frosty morning.

This is the way we go to school,
We go to school, we go to school,
This is the way we go to school,
On a cold and frosty morning.

Here we go round the mulberry bush,
The mulberry bush, the mulberry bush,
Here we go round the mulberry bush,
On a cold and frosty morning.

OLIVER TWIST

Oliver Twist
You can't do this,
So what's the use
Of trying?
Touch your toe,
Touch your knee,
Clap your hands,
Away we go.

A SAILOR WENT TO SEA

A sailor went to sea, sea, sea,
To see what he could see, see, see,
But all that he could see, see, see,
Was the bottom of the deep blue sea, sea, sea.

LITTLE SALLY WATERS

Little Sally Waters,
Sitting in the sun,
Crying and weeping,
For a young man.
Rise, Sally, rise,
Dry your weeping eyes,
Fly to the east,
Fly to the west,
Fly to the one you love the best.

MR. NOBODY

Mr. Nobody is a nice young man,
He comes to the door with his hat in his hand.
Down she comes, all dressed in silk,
A rose in her bosom, as white as milk.
She takes off her gloves, she shows me her ring,
Tomorrow, tomorrow, the wedding begins.

LONDON BRIDGE

London Bridge is falling down,
  Falling down, falling down;
London Bridge is falling down,
  My fair lady.

How shall we build it up again?
  Up again, up again;
How shall we build it up again?
  My fair lady.

Build it up with silver and gold,
  Silver and gold, silver and gold;
Build it up with silver and gold,
  My fair lady.

Silver and gold will be stole away,
  Stole away, stole away;
Silver and gold will be stole away,
  My fair lady.

Build it up with iron and steel,
　Iron and steel, iron and steel;
Build it up with iron and steel,
　My fair lady.

Iron and steel will bend and bow,
　Bend and bow, bend and bow;
Iron and steel will bend and bow,
　My fair lady.

Build it up with wood and clay,
　Wood and clay, wood and clay;
Build it up with wood and clay,
　My fair lady.

Wood and clay will wash away,
　Wash away, wash away;
Wood and clay will wash away,
　My fair lady.

Build it up with stone so strong,
　Stone so strong, stone so strong;
Huzza! 'twill last for ages long,
　My fair lady.

HAVE YOU SEEN THE MUFFIN MAN

Have you seen the muffin man, the muffin man, the
 muffin man,
Have you seen the muffin man that lives in Drury
 Lane O?
Yes, I've seen the muffin man, the muffin man, the
 muffin man;
Yes, I've seen the muffin man who lives in Drury
 Lane O.

OLD ROGER IS DEAD

Old Roger is dead and
  gone to his grave,
H'm ha! gone to his grave.

They planted an apple tree
  over his head,
H'm ha! over his head.

The apples were ripe
  and ready to fall,
H'm ha! ready to fall.

There came an old woman
  and picked them all up,
H'm ha! picked them all up.

Old Roger jumped up and
  gave her a knock,
H'm ha! gave her a knock.

Which made the old woman
  go hippity hop,
H'm ha! hippity hop!

23

HARK THE ROBBERS

Hark at the robbers going through,
   Through, through, through; through,
      through, through;
Hark at the robbers going through,
   My fair lady.

What have the robbers done to you,
   You, you, you; you, you, you?
What have the robbers done to you,
   My fair lady?

Stole my gold watch and chain,
   Chain, chain, chain; chain, chain, chain;
Stole my gold watch and chain,
   My fair lady.

How many pounds will set us free,
   Free, free, free; free, free, free?
How many pounds will set us free,
   My fair lady?

A hundred pounds will set you free,
   Free, free, free; free, free, free;

24

A hundred pounds will set you free,
    My fair lady.

We have not a hundred pounds,
    Pounds, pounds, pounds; pounds, pounds, pounds;
We have not a hundred pounds,
    My fair lady.

Then to prison you must go,
    Go, go, go; go, go, go;
Then to prison you must go,
    My fair lady.

To prison we will not go,
    Go, go, go; go, go, go;
To prison we will not go,
    My fair lady.

THE BELLS OF LONDON

Gay go up and gay go down,
To ring the bells of London town.

Halfpence and farthings,
Say the bells of St. Martin's.

Oranges and lemons,
Say the bells of St. Clement's.

Pancakes and fritters,
Say the bells of St. Peter's.

Two sticks and an apple,
Say the bells of Whitechapel.

Kettles and pans,
Say the bells of St. Ann's.

You owe me ten shillings,
Say the bells of St. Helen's.

When will you pay me?
Say the bells of Old Bailey.

When I grow rich,
Say the bells of Shoreditch.

Pray when will that be?
Say the bells of Stepney.

I am sure I don't know,
Says the great bell of Bow.

HERE COMES A WIDOW

Here comes a widow from Barbary-land,
With all her children in her hand;
One can brew, and one can bake,
And one can make a wedding-cake.
  Pray take one,
  Pray take two,
Pray take one that pleases you.

MISS MARY MACK

Miss Mary Mack, Mack, Mack,
All dressed in black, black, black,
With silver buttons, buttons, buttons,
All down her back, back, back.
She went upstairs to make her bed,
She made a mistake and bumped her head;
She went downstairs to wash the dishes,
She made a mistake and washed her wishes;
She went outside to hang her clothes,
She made a mistake and hung her nose.

SNEEZE ON MONDAY

Sneeze on Monday, sneeze for danger;
Sneeze on Tuesday, kiss a stranger;
Sneeze on Wednesday, get a letter;
Sneeze on Thursday, something better;
Sneeze on Friday, sneeze for sorrow;
Sneeze on Saturday, see your sweetheart
   tomorrow.

SEE A PIN AND PICK IT UP

See a pin and pick it up,
All the day you'll have good luck;
See a pin and let it lay,
Bad luck you'll have all the day!

RAIN, RAIN, GO AWAY

Rain, rain, go away,
Come again another day.

FIVE LITTLE MONKEYS

Five little monkeys walked along the shore;
One went a-sailing,
Then there were four.
Four little monkeys climbed up a tree;
One of them tumbled down,
Then there were three.
Three little monkeys found a pot of glue;
One got stuck in it,
Then there were two.
Two little monkeys found a currant bun;
One ran away with it,
Then there was one.
One little monkey cried all afternoon,
So they put him in an aeroplane
And sent him to the moon.

THREE CHILDREN

Three children sliding on the ice
   Upon a summer's day,
As it fell out, they all fell in,
   The rest they ran away.

Now had these children been at home,
   Or sliding on dry ground,
Ten thousand pounds to one penny
   They had not all been drowned.

You parents all that children have,
   And you that have got none,
If you would have them safe abroad,
   Pray keep them safe at home.

A FARMYARD SONG

I had a cat and the cat pleased me,
I fed my cat by yonder tree;
  Cat goes fiddle-i-fee.

I had a hen and the hen pleased me,
I fed my hen by yonder tree;
  Hen goes chimmy-chuck, chimmy-chuck,
  Cat goes fiddle-i-fee.

I had a duck and the duck pleased me,
I fed my duck by yonder tree;
    Duck goes quack, quack,
    Hen goes chimmy-chuck, chimmy-chuck,
    Cat goes fiddle-i-fee.

I had a goose and the goose pleased me,
I fed my goose by yonder tree;
    Goose goes swishy, swashy,
    Duck goes quack, quack,
    Hen goes chimmy-chuck, chimmy-chuck,
    Cat goes fiddle-i-fee.

I had a sheep and the sheep pleased me,
I fed my sheep by yonder tree;
 Sheep goes baa, baa,
 Goose goes swishy, swashy,
 Duck goes quack, quack,
 Hen goes chimmy-chuck, chimmy-chuck,
 Cat goes fiddle-i-fee.

I had a pig and the pig pleased me,
I fed my pig by yonder tree;
 Pig goes griffy, gruffy,
 Sheep goes baa, baa,
 Goose goes swishy, swashy,
 Duck goes quack, quack,
 Hen goes chimmy-chuck, chimmy-chuck,
 Cat goes fiddle-i-fee.

I had a cow and the cow pleased me,
I fed my cow by yonder tree;
   Cow goes moo, moo,
   Pig goes griffy, gruffy,
   Sheep goes baa, baa,
   Goose goes swishy, swashy,
   Duck goes quack, quack,
   Hen goes chimmy-chuck, chimmy-chuck,
   Cat goes fiddle-i-fee.

I had a horse and the horse pleased me,
I fed my horse by yonder tree;
  Horse goes neigh, neigh,
  Cow goes moo, moo,
  Pig goes griffy, gruffy,
  Sheep goes baa, baa,
  Goose goes swishy, swashy,
  Duck goes quack, quack,
  Hen goes chimmy-chuck, chimmy-chuck,
  Cat goes fiddle-i-fee.

I had a dog and the dog pleased me,
I fed my dog by yonder tree;
  Dog goes bow-wow, bow-wow,
  Horse goes neigh, neigh,
  Cow goes moo, moo,
  Pig goes griffy, gruffy,
  Sheep goes baa, baa,
  Goose goes swishy, swashy,
  Duck goes quack, quack,
  Hen goes chimmy-chuck, chimmy-chuck,
  Cat goes fiddle-i-fee.

HOW MANY DAYS HAS MY BABY TO PLAY?

How many days has my baby to play?
Saturday, Sunday, Monday;
Tuesday, Wednesday, Thursday, Friday,
Saturday, Sunday, Monday.

SING
A SONG
OF SIXPENCE

and

OTHER NONSENSE
RHYMES

SING A SONG OF SIXPENCE

Sing a song of sixpence,
  A pocket full of rye;
Four and twenty blackbirds,
  Baked in a pie.

When the pie was opened,
  The birds began to sing;
Was not that dainty dish,
  To set before the king?

The king was in his counting-house,
   Counting out his money;
The queen was in the parlour,
   Eating bread and honey.

The maid was in the garden,
   Hanging out the clothes,
There came a little blackbird,
   And snapped off her nose.

I LOVE SIXPENCE

I love sixpence, pretty little sixpence,
  I love sixpence better than my life;
I spent a penny of it, I spent another,
  And took fourpence home to my wife.

Oh, my little fourpence, pretty little fourpence,
  I love fourpence better than my life;
I spent a penny of it, I spent another,
  And I took twopence home to my wife.

Oh, my little twopence, my pretty little twopence,
  I love twopence better than my life;
I spent a penny of it, I spent another,
  And I took nothing home to my wife.

Oh, my little nothing, my pretty little nothing,
  What will nothing buy for my wife?
I have nothing, I spend nothing,
  I love nothing better than my wife.

THE MILLER OF DEE

There was a jolly miller
   Lived on the river Dee:
He worked and sung from morn till night,
   No lark so blithe as he;
And this the burden of his song
   For ever used to be—
I jump mejerrime jee!
   I care for nobody—no! not I,
Since nobody cares for me.

AS I WAS GOING ALONG

As I was going along, long, long,

A singing a comical song, song, song,

The lane that I went was so long, long, long,

And the song that I sung was as long, long, long,

And so I went singing along.

OVER THE HILLS AND FAR AWAY

When I was young and had no sense
I bought a fiddle for eighteenpence,
And the only tune that I could play
Was "Over the Hills and Far Away".

HEY, DIDDLE, DIDDLE

Hey, diddle, diddle, the cat and the fiddle,
The cow jumped over the moon;
The little dog laughed to see such sport,
And the dish ran away with the spoon!

ONE, TWO, BUCKLE MY SHOE

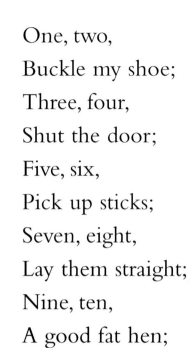

One, two,
Buckle my shoe;
Three, four,
Shut the door;
Five, six,
Pick up sticks;
Seven, eight,
Lay them straight;
Nine, ten,
A good fat hen;

Eleven, twelve,
Who will delve?
Thirteen, fourteen,
Maids a-courting;
Fifteen, sixteen,
Maids a-kissing;
Seventeen, eighteen,
Maid a-waiting;
Nineteen, twenty,
My stomach's empty.

GOOSEY, GOOSEY, GANDER

Goosey, goosey, gander,
 Whither shall I wander,
Upstairs, and downstairs,
 And in my lady's chamber.
There I met an old man,
 Who would not say his prayers,
I took him by his left leg
 And threw him down the stairs.

DAFFY-DOWN-DILLY

Daffy-
Down-
Dilly
has come
up to
town

In a
yellow
petticoat
and a
green
gown.

FROM WIBBLETON TO WOBBLETON

From Wibbleton to Wobbleton
  is fifteen miles,
From Wobbleton to Wibbleton
  is fifteen miles,
From Wibbleton to Wobbleton,
From Wobbleton to Wibbleton,
From Wibbleton to Wobbleton
  is fifteen miles.

SEE-SAW, SACRADOWN

See-saw, Sacradown,
Which is the way to London Town?
One foot up and one foot down,
That's the way to London Town.

HUMPTY DUMPTY

Humpty Dumpty sat on a wall,
Humpty Dumpty had a great fall;
All the king's horses and all the king's men
Couldn't put Humpty together again.

TWEEDLE-DUM AND TWEEDLE-DEE

Tweedle-dum and Tweedle-dee
    Agreed to have a battle,
For Tweedle-dum said Tweedle-dee
    Had spoiled his nice new rattle.
Just then flew down a monstrous crow,
    As big as a tar-barrel,
Which frightened both the heroes so,
    They quite forgot their quarrel.

ROBIN THE BOBBIN

Robin the Bobbin, the big-bellied Ben,
He ate more meat than fourscore men;
He ate a cow, he ate a calf,
He ate a butcher and a half;
He ate a church, he ate a steeple,
He ate the priest and all the people!
    A cow and a calf,
    An ox and a half,
    A church and a steeple,
    And all the good people,
And yet he complained that his stomach wasn't full.

HECTOR PROTECTOR

Hector Protector was dressed all in green;

Hector Protector was sent to the Queen.

The Queen did not like him,

Nor more did the King;

So Hector Protector was sent back again.

THE LION AND THE UNICORN

The lion and the unicorn
　　Were fighting for the crown:
The lion beat the unicorn
　　All round the town.
Some gave them white bread,
　　Some gave them brown:
Some gave them plum-cake
　　And drummed them out of town.

60

POP GOES THE WEASEL

Up and down the City Road
In and out the Eagle,
That's the way the money goes,
Pop goes the weasel!

Half a pound of tuppenny rice,
Half a pound of treacle,
Mix it up and make it nice,
Pop goes the weasel!

Every night when I go out
The monkey's on the table;
Take a stick and knock it off,
Pop goes the weasel!

BLOW, WIND, BLOW!

Blow, wind, blow! and go, mill, go!
That the miller may grind his corn;
That the baker may take it,
And into rolls make it,
And send us some hot in the morn.

PAT-A-CAKE, PAT-A-CAKE
BAKER'S MAN!

Pat-a-cake, pat-a-cake, baker's man!
Bake me a cake, as fast as you can;
Pat it and prick it, and mark it with T,
And put it aside for Tommy and me.

HOT-CROSS BUNS

Hot-Cross Buns!
Hot-Cross Buns!
One a penny, two a penny,
Hot-Cross Buns!

Hot-Cross Buns!
Hot-Cross Buns!
If you have no daughters
Give them to your sons.

PEASE-PUDDING HOT

Pease-pudding hot,
  Pease-pudding cold,
Pease-pudding in the pot,
  Nine days old.
Some like it hot,
  Some like it cold,
Some like it in the pot,
  Nine days old.

THE MAN IN THE MOON

The man in the moon,
  Came tumbling down,
And asked his way to Norwich.
  He went by the south,
  And burnt his mouth
With supping cold pease-porridge.

HIGGLETY, PIGGLETY, POP!

Higglety, pigglety, pop!
The dog has eaten the mop;
The pig's in a hurry,
The cat's in a flurry,
Higglety, pigglety, pop!

WE'RE ALL IN THE DUMPS

We're all in the dumps,
For diamonds and trumps,
The kittens are gone to St. Paul's,
The babies are bit,
The moon's in a fit,
And the houses are built without walls.

RING-A-RING O' ROSES

Ring-a ring o' roses
A pocket full of posies,
A-tishoo! A-tishoo!
We all fall down.

MY FATHER DIED, BUT I CAN'T TELL YOU HOW

My father he died, but I can't tell you how,
He left me six horses to drive in my plough:
    With my wing wang waddle oh,
    Jack sing saddle oh,
    Blowsey boys buble oh,
    Under the broom.

I sold my six horses and I bought me a cow,
I'd fain have made a fortune but did not know how:
    With my wing wang waddle oh,
    Jack sing saddle oh,
    Blowsey boys buble oh,
    Under the broom.

I sold my cow, and I bought me a calf;
I'd fain have made a fortune but lost the best half:
    With my wing wang waddle oh,
    Jack sing saddle oh,
    Blowsey boys buble oh,
    Under the broom.

I sold my calf, and I bought me a cat;
A pretty thing she was, in my chimney corner sat:
  With my wing wang waddle oh,
  Jack sing saddle oh,
  Blowsey boys buble oh,
  Under the broom.

I sold my cat, and bought me a mouse;
He carried fire in his tail, and burnt down my house:
  With my wing wang waddle oh,
  Jack sing saddle oh,
  Blowsey boys buble oh,
  Under the broom.

IF ALL THE SEAS WERE ONE SEA

If all the seas were one sea,
What a *great* sea that would be!
And if all the trees were one tree,
What a *great* tree that would be!
And if all the axes were one axe,
What a *great* axe that would be!
And if all the men were one man,
What a *great* man he would be!
And if the *great* man took the *great* axe,
And cut down the *great* tree,
And let it fall into the *great* sea,
What a splish splash *that* would be!

LITTLE
BOY BLUE

and

OTHER RHYMES
OF CHILDHOOD

LITTLE BOY BLUE

Little Boy Blue,
　　Come blow your horn,
The sheep's in the meadow,
　　The cow's in the corn.

Where is the boy
　　Who looks after the sheep?
He's under a haycock
　　Fast asleep.
Will you wake him?
　　No, not I,
For if I do,
　　He's sure to cry.

THERE WAS A LITTLE BOY

There was a little boy went into a barn,
And lay down on some hay;
An owl came out and flew about,
And the little boy ran away.

ROBIN AND RICHARD

Robin and Richard were two pretty men;
They laid in bed till the clock struck ten;
Then up starts Robin and looks at the sky,
Oh! brother Richard, the sun's very high:

The bull's in the barn threshing the corn,
The cock's on the dunghill blowing his horn,
The cat's at the fire frying of fish,
The dog's in the pantry breaking his dish.

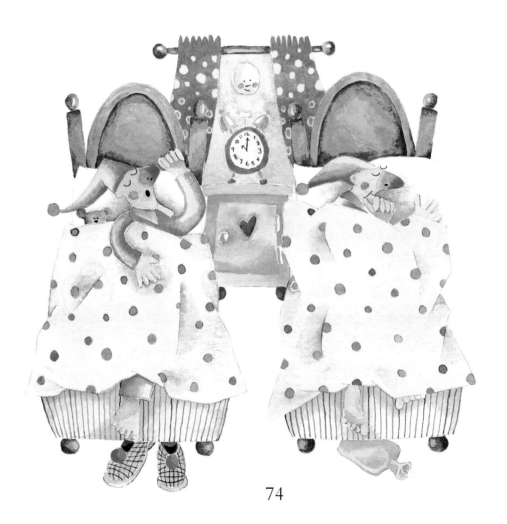

LITTLE TOMMY TITTLEMOUSE

Little Tommy Tittlemouse
Lived in a little house;
He caught fishes
In other men's ditches.

SEE-SAW, MARGERY DAW

See-saw, Margery Daw,
Jack shall have a new master;
He shall have but a penny a day,
Because he can't work any faster.

JACK, JACK, THE BREAD'S A-BURNING

Jack, Jack, the bread's a-burning,
All to a cinder;
If you don't come and fetch it out
We'll throw it through the window.

JACK AND GUY

Jack and Guy
  Went out in the rye,
And they found a little boy with one black eye.
Come, says Jack, let's knock him on the head.
No, says Guy, let's buy him some bread;
You buy one loaf and I'll buy two,
And we'll bring him up as other folk do.

JACK AND JILL

Jack and Jill went up the hill
    To fetch a pail of water;
Jack fell down and broke his crown,
    And Jill came tumbling after.

Up Jack got, and home did trot,
    As fast as he could caper,
Went to bed to mend his head
    With vinegar and brown paper.

LITTLE JACK JINGLE

Little Jack Jingle,
He used to live single:
But when he got tired of this kind of life,
He left off being single, and lived with his wife.

HARRY PARRY

O rare Harry Parry,
When will you marry?
When apples and pears are ripe.
I'll come to your wedding,
Without any bidding,
And dance and sing all the night.

YOUNG ROGER CAME TAPPING

Young Roger came tapping at Dolly's window,
  Thumpaty, thumpaty, thump!
He asked for admittance, she answered him "No!"
  Frumpaty, frumpaty, frump!

"No, no, Roger, no! as you came you may go!"
  Stumpaty, stumpaty, stump!

BOBBIE SHAFTOE'S GONE TO SEA

Bobbie Shaftoe's gone to sea,
Silver buckles at his knee;
When he comes back he'll marry me,
Bonny Bobbie Shaftoe!

JOHNNY SHALL HAVE A NEW BONNET

Johnny shall have a new bonnet,
And Johnny shall go to the fair,
And Johnny shall have a blue ribbon
To tie up his bonny brown hair.

PETER, PETER, PUMPKIN EATER

Peter, Peter, pumpkin eater,
Had a wife and couldn't keep her;
He put her in a pumpkin shell
And there he kept her very well.

Peter, Peter, pumpkin eater,
Had another and didn't love her;
Peter learned to read and spell,
And then he loved her very well.

SIMPLE SIMON

Simple Simon met a pieman
  Going to the fair;
Said Simple Simon to the pieman,
  "Let me taste your ware."

Said the pieman to Simple Simon,
  "Show me first your penny";
Said Simple Simon to the pieman,
  "Indeed I have not any."

LITTLE JACK HORNER

Little Jack Horner
Sat in a corner,
Eating his Christmas pie;
He put in his thumb,
And pulled out a plum,
And said: "What a good boy am I!"

WHEN JACKY'S A VERY GOOD BOY

When Jacky's a very good boy,
He shall have cakes and a custard;
But when he does nothing but cry,
He shall have nothing but mustard

LITTLE TOMMY TUCKER

Little Tommy Tucker
  Sings for his supper:
What shall we give him?
  Brown bread and butter.
How shall he cut it
  Without a knife?
How can he marry
  Without a wife?

TOM, TOM, THE PIPER'S SON

Tom, Tom, the piper's son,
Stole a pig, and away he run.
The pig was eat, and Tom was beat,
And Tom went roaring down the street.

TOM, HE WAS A PIPER'S SON

Tom, he was a piper's son,
He learnt to play when he was young,
And all the tune that he could play,
Was, "Over the hills and far away."

Over the hills and a great way off,
The wind shall blow my topknot off.

Tom with his pipe made such a noise
That he pleased both the girls and boys,
And they all stopped to hear him play
"Over the hills and far away."

Over the hills and a great way off,
The wind shall blow my topknot off.

TOMMY SNOOKS AND BESSY BROOKS

As Tommy Snooks and Bessy Brooks
Were walking out one Sunday,
Says Tommy Snooks to Bessy Brooks,
"Tomorrow will be Monday."

LITTLE JUMPING JOAN

Here am I, little jumping Joan.
When nobody's with me,
I'm always alone.

THERE WAS A LITTLE GIRL

There was a little girl, and she had a little curl
    Right in the middle of her forehead;
When she was good she was very, very good,
    But when she was bad she was horrid.

ANNA BANANA

Anna Banana
Played the piano;
The piano broke
And Anna choked.

LUCY LOCKET

Lucy Locket lost her pocket,
  Kitty Fisher found it,
But not a penny was there in it
  Just the binding round it

LITTLE MISS MUFFET

Little Miss Muffet

Sat on a tuffet,

Eating her curds and whey;

There came a great spider,

Who sat down beside her,

And frightened Miss Muffet away.

ELSIE MARLEY

Elsie Marley is grown so fine,
She won't get up to serve the swine,
But lies in bed till eight or nine,
And surely she does take her time.

MARY, MARY

Mary, Mary, quite contrary,
How does your garden grow?
With silver bells, and cockle shells,
And pretty maids all in a row.

POLLY, PUT THE KETTLE ON

Polly, put the kettle on,
Polly, put the kettle on,
Polly, put the kettle on,
   And we'll all have tea.

Sukey, take it off again,
Sukey, take it off again,
Sukey, take it off again,
   They're all gone away.

A PRETTY LITTLE GIRL

A pretty little girl in a round-eared cap
I met in the streets the other day;
  She gave me such a thump,
  That my heart it went bump;
I thought I should have fainted away!
I thought I should have fainted away!

GILLY SILLY JARTER

Gilly Silly Jarter,
Who has lost a garter?
In a shower of rain,
The miller found it,
The miller ground it,
And the miller gave it to Silly again.

MR. PUNCHINELLO

Oh! mother, I shall be married to Mr. Punchinello.
   To Mr. Punch,
   To Mr. Joe,
   To Mr. Nell,
   To Mr. Lo,
   Mr. Punch, Mr. Joe,
   Mr. Nell, Mr. Lo,
   To Mr. Punchinello.

GOLDY LOCKS, GOLDY LOCKS

Goldy locks, goldy locks,
  Wilt thou be mine?
Thou shalt not wash dishes,
  Nor yet feed the swine;

But sit on a cushion,
  And sew a fine seam,
And feed upon strawberries,
  Sugar and cream.

LAVENDER'S BLUE

Lilies are white,
Rosemary's green;
When you are king,
I will be queen.

Roses are red,
Lavender's blue;
If you will have me,
I will have you.

MONDAY'S CHILD IS FAIR OF FACE

Monday's child is fair of face,
Tuesday's child is full of grace,
Wednesday's child is full of woe,
Thursday's child has far to go,
Friday's child is loving and giving,
Saturday's child works hard for his living,
And the child that is born on the Sabbath day
Is bonny and blithe, and good and gay.

BAA, BAA,
BLACK SHEEP

and

OTHER ANIMAL
RHYMES

BAA, BAA, BLACK SHEEP

Baa, baa, black sheep, have you any wool?
Yes, sir; yes, sir, three bags full:
One for the master, one for the dame,
And one for the little boy that lives down the lane.

MARY HAD A LITTLE LAMB

Mary had a little lamb,
Its fleece was white as snow,
And everywhere that Mary went
The lamb was sure to go.

It followed her to school one day,
Which was against the rule;
It made the children laugh and play
To see a lamb in school.

CUSHY COW BONNY

Cushy cow bonny, let down thy milk,
And I will give thee a gown of silk;
A gown of silk and a silver tree,
If thou wilt let down thy milk to me.

I HAD A LITTLE COW

I had a little cow;
  Hey-diddle, ho-diddle!
I had a little cow, and it had a little calf;
Hey-diddle, ho-diddle; and there's my song half.

I had a little cow;
  Hey-diddle, ho-diddle!
I had a little cow, and I drove it to the stall;
Hey-diddle, ho-diddle; and there's my song all!

THERE WAS A PIPER,
HE'D A COW

There was a piper, he'd a cow,
   And he'd no hay to give her;
He took his pipes and played a tune:
   "Consider, old cow, consider!"

The cow considered very well,
   For she gave the piper a penny,
That he might play the tune again,
   Of "Corn rigs are bonnie".

WAY DOWN YONDER IN THE MAPLE SWAMP

Way down yonder in the maple swamp
The wild geese gather and the ganders honk
The mares kick up and the ponies prance;
The old sow whistles and the little pigs dance.

BETTY PRINGLE

Betty Pringle had a little pig,
Not very little and not very big;
When he was alive he lived in clover;
But now he's dead, and that's all over.
So Billy Pringle he laid down and cried,
And Betty Pringle she laid down and died;
So there was an end of one, two, and three:
Billy Pringle he,
Betty Pringle she,
And the piggy wiggy.

TIGGY-TOUCHWOOD

Tiggy-tiggy-touchwood, my black hen,
She lays eggs for gentlemen,
Sometimes nine and sometimes ten,
Tiggy-tiggy-touchwood, my black hen.

I HAD A LITTLE HEN

I had a little hen, the prettiest ever seen,
She washed me the dishes, and kept the house clean:
She went to the mill to fetch me some flour,
She brought it home in less than an hour;
She baked me my bread, she brewed me my ale,
She sat by the fire and told many a fine tale.

MRS HEN

Chook, chook, chook, chook, chook,
   Good morning, Mrs Hen.
How many chickens have you got?
   Madam, I've got ten.

Four of them are yellow,
   And four of them are brown,
And two of them are speckled red,
   The nicest in the town.

A SWARM OF BEES IN MAY

A swarm of bees in May
Is worth a load of hay;
A swarm of bees in June
Is worth a silver spoon;
A swarm of bees in July
Is not worth a fly.

INCEY WINCEY SPIDER

Incey Wincey spider
　　Climbing up the spout;
Down came the rain
　　And washed the spider out:
Out came the sunshine
　　And dried up all the rain;
Incey Wincey spider
　　Climbing up again.

BOW, WOW, WOW

Bow, wow, wow,
　Whose dog art thou?
"Little Tom Tinker's dog,
　Bow, wow, wow."

TWO LITTLE DOGS

Two little dogs
Sat by the fire
Over a fender of coal-dust;
Said one little dog
To the other little dog,
If you don't talk, why, I must.

PUSSY-CAT SITS BY THE FIRE

Pussy-cat sits by the fire.
   How did she come there?
In walks the little dog,
   Says, "Pussy! are you there?
How do you do, Mistress Pussy?
   Mistress Pussy, how d'ye do?"
"I thank you kindly, little dog,
   I fare as well as you!"

I LOVE LITTLE PUSSY

I love little pussy, her coat is so warm;
And if I don't hurt her she'll do me no harm.
So I'll not pull her tail nor drive her away,
But pussy and I very gently will play.

PUSSY-CAT MOLE

Pussy-cat Mole,
Jumped over a coal,
And in her best petticoat burnt a great hole.
Poor pussy's weeping, she'll have no more milk,
Until her best petticoat's mended with silk.

PUSSY-CAT, PUSSY-CAT

Pussy-cat, pussy-cat, where have you been?
I've been to London to see the Queen.
Pussy-cat, pussy-cat, what did you there?
I frightened a little mouse under her chair.

THREE LITTLE KITTENS

Three little kittens they lost their mittens,
  And they began to cry,
Oh, mother dear, we sadly fear
  That we have lost our mittens.
What! lost your mittens, you naughty kittens!
  Then you shall have no pie.
  Mee-ow, mee-ow, mee-ow.
  No, you shall have no pie.

The three little kittens they found their mittens,
  And they began to cry,
Oh, mother dear, see here, see here,
  For we have found our mittens.
Put on your mittens, you silly kittens,
  And you shall have some pie.
  Purr-r, purr-r, purr-r,
  Oh, let us have some pie.

The three little kittens put on their mittens,
  And soon ate up the pie;
Oh, mother dear, we greatly fear
  That we have soiled our mittens.
What! soiled your mittens, you naughty kittens!
  Then they began to sigh.
  Mee-ow, mee-ow, mee-ow.
  Then they began to sigh.

The three little kittens they washed their mittens,
  And hung them out to dry;
Oh! mother dear, do you not hear
  That we have washed our mittens?
What! washed your mittens, then you're good kittens,
  But I smell a rat close by.
  Mee-ow, mee-ow, mee-ow.
  We smell a rat close by.

THREE YOUNG RATS

Three young rats with black felt hats,
Three young ducks with white straw flats,
Three young dogs with curling tails,
Three young cats with demi-veils,
Went out to walk with two young pigs
In satin vests and sorrel wigs;
But suddenly it chanced to rain,
And so they all went home again.

THE COLD OLD HOUSE

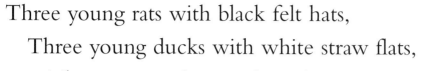

I know a house, and a cold old house,
A cold old house by the sea.
If I were a mouse in that cold old house
What a cold cold mouse I'd be!

118

THREE BLIND MICE

Three blind mice, see how they run!
Three blind mice, see how they run!
  They all ran after the farmer's wife,
Who cut off their tails with a carving-knife,
Did ever you hear such a thing in your life,
  As three blind mice.

BAT, BAT

Bat, Bat, come under my hat,
  And I'll give you a slice of bacon,
And when I bake I'll give you a cake,
  If I am not mistaken.

HICKORY, DICKORY, DOCK

Hickory, dickory, dock,
The mouse ran up the clock.
The clock struck one,
The mouse ran down,
Hickory, dickory, dock.

INTERY, MINTERY, CUTERY, CORN

Intery, mintery, cutery, corn,

Apple seed and apple thorn.

Wire, briar, limber, lock,

Three geese in a flock.

One flew east and one flew west;

One flew over the cuckoo's nest.

THE CUCKOO

Cuckoo, Cuckoo,
What do you do?
In April
I open my bill;
In May
I sing night and day;
In June
I change my tune;
In July
Away I fly;
In August
Away I must.

MAGPIES

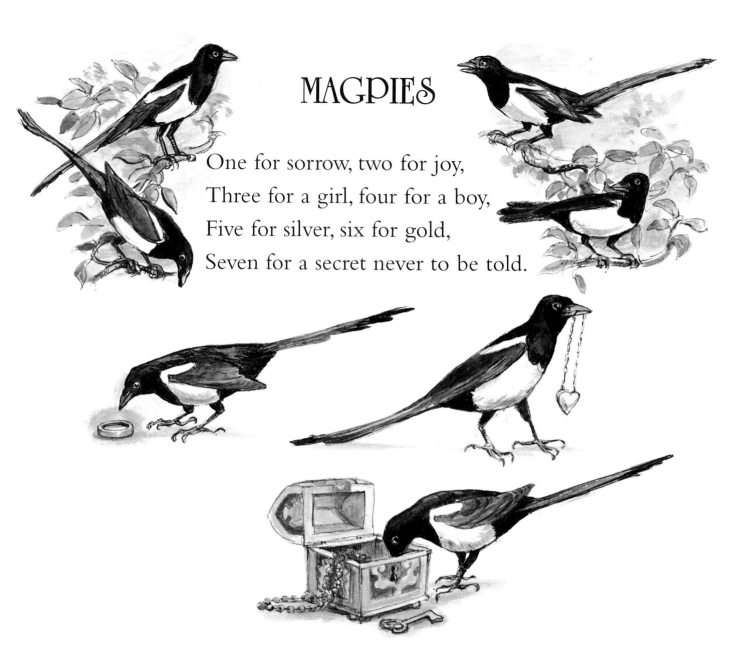

One for sorrow, two for joy,
Three for a girl, four for a boy,
Five for silver, six for gold,
Seven for a secret never to be told.

LITTLE ROBIN REDBREAST

Little Robin Redbreast
  Sat upon a rail:
Niddle-noddle went his head!
  Wiggle-waggle went his tail.

THE NORTH WIND DOTH BLOW

The north wind doth blow,
And we shall have snow,
And what will poor Robin do then?
                    Poor thing!

He'll sit in a barn,
And to keep himself warm,
Will hide his head under his wing.
                    Poor thing!

ONCE I SAW A LITTLE BIRD

Once I saw a little bird
Come hop, hop, hop;
So I cried, "Little bird,
Will you stop, stop, stop?"
And was going to the window,
To say, "How do you do?"
But he shook his little tail,
And far away he flew.

JAY-BIRD

Jay-bird, jay-bird, settin' on a rail,
Pickin' his teeth with the end of his tail;
Mulberry leaves and calico sleeves—
All school teachers are hard to please.

BIRDS OF A FEATHER

Birds of a feather flock together
And so will pigs and swine;
Rats and mice shall have their choice,
And so shall I have mine.

THERE WERE TWO BIRDS SAT ON A STONE

There were two birds sat on a stone,
  Fa, la, la, la, lal, de;
One flew away, then there was one,
  Fa, la, la, la, lal, de;
The other flew after, and then there
    was none,
  Fa, la, la, la, lal, de;
And so the poor stone was left all alone,
  Fa, la, la, la, lal, de!

TWO LITTLE DICKY BIRDS

Two little dicky birds sitting on a wall,
One named Peter, one named Paul.
  Fly away, Peter!
  Fly away, Paul!
    Come back, Peter!
    Come back, Paul!

THE WISE OLD OWL

There was an old owl who lived in an oak;
The more he heard, the less he spoke.
The less he spoke, the more he heard.
Why aren't we like that wise old bird!

THERE WAS AN OLD CROW

There was an old crow
Sat upon a clod:
There's an end of my song,
That's odd!

THE
HOUSE THAT JACK
BUILT

and

OTHER STORY
RHYMES

THE HOUSE THAT JACK BUILT

This is the house that Jack built.

This is the malt
That lay in the house that Jack built.

This is the rat,
That ate the malt,
That lay in the house that Jack built.

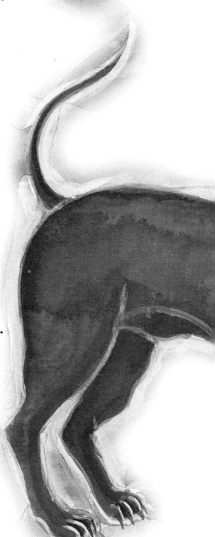

This is the cat,
That killed the rat,
That ate the malt,
That lay in the house that Jack built.

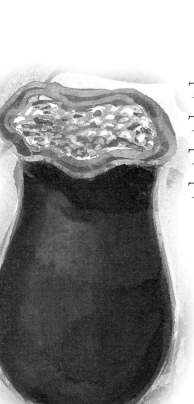

This is the dog,
That worried the cat,
That killed the rat,
That ate the malt,
That lay in the house that Jack built.

This is the cow with the crumpled horn,
That tossed the dog,
That worried the cat,
That killed the rat,
That ate the malt,
That lay in the house that Jack built.

133

This is the maiden all forlorn,
That milked the cow with the crumpled horn,
That tossed the dog,
That worried the cat,
That killed the rat,
That ate the malt,
That lay in the house that Jack built.

This is the man all tattered and torn,
That kissed the maiden all forlorn,
That milked the cow with the crumpled horn,
That tossed the dog,
That worried the cat,
That killed the rat,
That ate the malt,
That lay in the house that Jack built.

This is the priest all shaven and shorn,

That married the man all tattered and torn,

That kissed the maiden all forlorn,

That milked the cow with the crumpled horn,

That tossed the dog,

That worried the cat,

That killed the rat,

That ate the malt,

That lay in the house that Jack built.

This is the cock that crowed in the morn,
That waked the priest all shaven and shorn,
That married the man all tattered and torn,
That kissed the maiden all forlorn,
That milked the cow with the crumpled horn,
That tossed the dog,
That worried the cat,
That killed the rat,
That ate the malt,
That lay in the house that Jack built.

This is the farmer sowing his corn,

That kept the cock that crowed in the morn,

That waked the priest all shaven and shorn,

That married the man all tattered and torn,

That kissed the maiden all forlorn,

That milked the cow with the crumpled horn,

That tossed the dog,

That worried the cat,

That killed the rat,

That ate the malt,

That lay in the house that Jack built.

A CAT CAME FIDDLING OUT OF A BARN

A cat came fiddling out of a barn,

With a pair of bagpipes under her arm;

She could sing nothing but fiddle cum fee,

The mouse has married the humble-bee.

Pipe, cat—dance, mouse,

We'll have a wedding at our good house.

DING, DONG, BELL

Ding, dong, bell,
Pussy's in the well.
  Who put her in?
  Little Tommy Green.
Who pulled her out?
Little Tommy Trout.
  What a naughty boy was that,
  To try and drown poor pussy cat.
Who never did him any harm,
And killed the mice in his Father's barn.

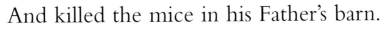

LITTLE BO-PEEP

Little Bo-peep has lost her sheep,
   And can't tell where to find them;
Leave them alone, and they'll come home,
   And bring their tails behind them.

Little Bo-peep fell fast asleep,
   And dreamt she heard them bleating;
But when she awoke, she found it a joke,
   For they were still a-fleeting.

Then up she took her little crook,
  Determined for to find them;
She found them indeed, but it made her
    heart bleed,
    For they'd left all their tails behind'em.

It happened one day, as Bo-peep did stray
  Under a meadow hard by:
There she espied their tails side by side,
  All hung on a tree to dry.

FOLLOW MY BANGALOREY MAN

Follow my Bangalorey Man,
Follow my Bangalorey Man;
I'll do all that ever I can
To follow my Bangalorey Man.
We'll borrow a horse, and steal a gig,
And round the world we'll do a jig,
And I'll do all that ever I can
To follow my Bangalorey Man!

ANNA MARIA

Anna Maria she sat on the fire;

The fire was too hot, she sat on the pot;

The pot was too round, she sat on the ground;

The ground was too flat, she sat on the cat;

The cat ran away with Maria on her back.

HANDY SPANDY, JACK-A-DANDY

Handy Spandy, Jack-a-dandy
Loved plum-cake and sugar-candy;
He bought some at a grocer's shop,
And out he came, hop, hop, hop.

YANKEE DOODLE

Yankee Doodle went to town,
Riding on a pony;
He stuck a feather in his hat,
And called it macaroni.
    Yankee Doodle fa, so, la,
    Yankee Doodle dandy,
    Yankee Doodle fa, so, la,
    Buttermilk and brandy.

Yankee Doodle went to town
To buy a pair of trousers,
He swore he could not see the town
For so many houses.
    Yankee Doodle fa, so, la,
    Yankee Doodle dandy,
    Yankee Doodle fa, so, la,
    Buttermilk and brandy.

HARK! HARK!

Hark, hark,
The dogs do bark,
Beggars are coming to town:
Some in rags,
Some in tags,
And some in velvet gowns.

IF WISHES WERE HORSES

If wishes were horses,
  Beggars would ride;
If turnips were watches,
  I'd wear one by my side.

IF ALL THE WORLD WAS APPLE-PIE

If all the world was apple-pie,
　And all the sea was ink,
And all the trees were bread and cheese,
　What should we have for drink?

FOR WANT OF A NAIL

For want of a nail, the shoe was lost;
For want of the shoe, the horse was lost;
For want of the horse, the rider was lost;
For want of the rider, the battle was lost;
For want of the battle, the kingdom was lost;
And all from the want of a horseshoe nail.

WHEN FAMED KING ARTHUR RULED THIS LAND

When famed King Arthur ruled this land
  He was a goodly king:
He took three pecks of barley meal
  To make a bag pudding.

A rare pudding the king did make,
  And stuffed it well with plums;
And in it put such lumps of fat,
  As big as my two thumbs.

The king and queen did eat thereof,
  And noblemen beside,
And what they could not eat that night
  The queen next morning fried.

WHAT IS THE RHYME FOR PORRINGER?

What is the rhyme for *porringer*?
The King he had a daughter fair,
And gave the Prince of Orange her.

GREY GOOSE AND GANDER

Grey goose and gander,
  Waft your wings together,
And carry the good king's daughter
  Over the one strand river.

I SAW THREE SHIPS

I saw three ships come sailing by,
    Come sailing by, come sailing by;
I saw three ships come sailing by,
    On New Year's Day in the morning.

And what do you think was in them then,
    Was in them then, was in them then?
And what do you think was in them then,
    On New Year's Day in the morning?

Three pretty girls were in them then,
    Were in them then, were in them then;
Three pretty girls were in them then,
    On New Year's Day in the morning.

And one could whistle, and one could sing,
    And one could play on the violin—
Such joy there was at my wedding,
    On New Year's Day in the morning.

I SAW A SHIP A-SAILING

I saw a ship a-sailing,
   A-sailing on the sea;
And, oh! it was all laden
   With pretty things for thee!

There were comfits in the cabin,
   And apples in the hold
The sails were made of silk,
   And the masts were made of gold.

The four-and-twenty sailors
   That stood between the decks,
Were four-and-twenty white mice
   With chains about their necks.

The captain was a duck,
   With a packet on his back;
And when the ship began to move,
   The captain said, "Quack! quack!"

THE MAN IN THE WILDERNESS

The man in the Wilderness asked me,
How many strawberries grew in the sea?
I answered him as I thought good,
As many red herrings as grew in the wood.

A PEANUT SAT ON THE RAILROAD TRACK

A peanut sat on the railroad track,
His heart was all a-flutter;
Along came a train—the 9:15—
Toot, toot, peanut butter!

THE QUEEN OF HEARTS

The Queen of Hearts, she made some tarts,
   All on a summer's day;
The Knave of Hearts, he stole the tarts,
   And took them clean away.

The King of Hearts called for the tarts,
   And beat the Knave full sore;
The Knave of Hearts brought back the tarts,
   And vowed he'd steal no more.

THE THREE JOVIAL WELSHMEN

There were three jovial Welshmen,
　As I have heard them say,
And they would go a-hunting
　Upon St. David's day.

All the day they hunted,
　And nothing could they find
But a ship a-sailing,
　A-sailing with the wind.

One said it was a ship;
　The other he said nay;
The third said it was a house,
　With the chimney blown away.

And all the night they hunted,
  And nothing could they find
But the moon a-gliding,
  A-gliding with the wind.

One said it was the moon;
  The other he said nay;
The third said it was a cheese,
  And half of it cut away.

And all the day they hunted,
  And nothing could they find
But a hedgehog in a bramble-bush,
  And that they left behind.

The first said it was hedgehog;
  The second he said nay;
The third it was a pin-cushion,
  And the pins stuck in wrong way.

And all the night they hunted,
  And nothing could they find
But a hare in a turnip field,
  And that they left behind.

The first said it was a hare;
  The second he said nay;
The third said it was a calf,
  And the cow had run away.

And all the day they hunted,
   And nothing could they find
But an owl in a holly-tree,
   And that they left behind.

One said it was an owl;
   The other he said nay;
The third it was an old man,
   And his beard growing grey.

FIRE ON THE MOUNTAIN

Rats in the garden—catch'em Towser!
Cows in the cornfield—run boys run!
Cat's in the cream pot—stop her now, sir!
Fire on the mountain—run boys run!

BILLY BOOSTER

Billy Billy Booster,
Had a little rooster,
The rooster died
And Billy cried.
Poor Billy Booster.

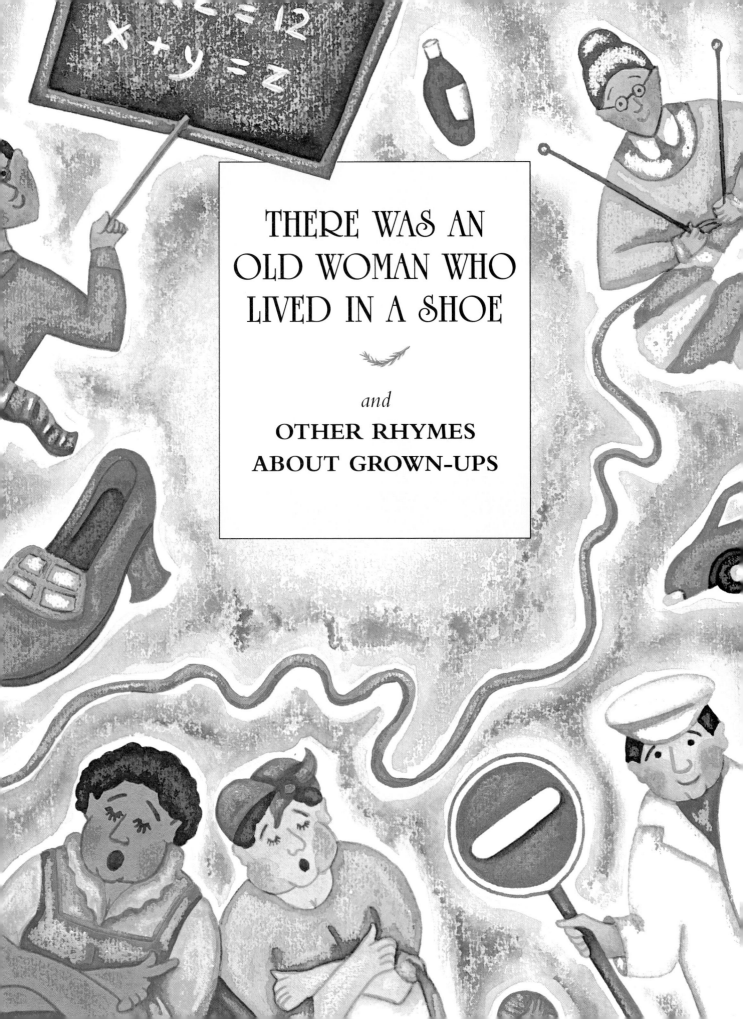

THERE WAS AN OLD WOMAN WHO LIVED IN A SHOE

and

OTHER RHYMES ABOUT GROWN-UPS

THERE WAS AN OLD WOMAN
WHO LIVED IN A SHOE

There was an old woman who lived in a shoe,
She had so many children she didn't know
  what to do;
She gave them some broth without any bread;
And scolded them soundly and put them to bed.

THERE WAS AN OLD WOMAN AND WHAT DO YOU THINK?

There was an old woman, and what do you think?
She lived upon nothing but victuals and drink:
Victuals and drink were the chief of her diet;
This tiresome old woman could never be quiet.

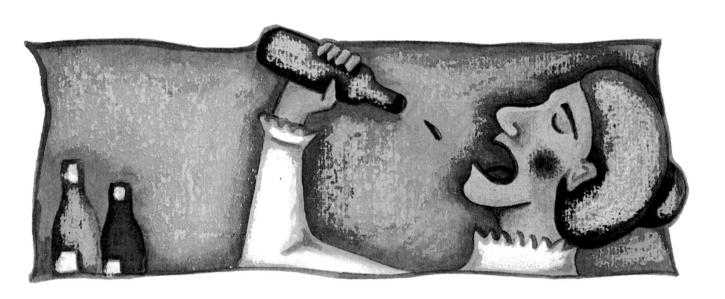

THERE WAS AN OLD WOMAN CALLED NOTHING-AT-ALL

There was an old woman called Nothing-at-all,
Who rejoiced in a dwelling exceedingly small;
A man stretched his mouth to its utmost extent,
And down at one gulp house and old woman went.

THERE WAS AN OLD WOMAN
LIVED UNDER A HILL

There was old woman
Lived under a hill,
And if she's not gone
She lives there still.

THERE WAS AN OLD WOMAN
HAD THREE SONS

There was an old woman had three sons,
Jerry, and James, and John:
Jerry was hung, James was drowned,
John was lost and never was found,
And there was an end of the three sons,
Jerry, and James, and John!

THERE WAS AN OLD WOMAN
WENT UP IN A BASKET

There was an old woman went up in a basket,
Seventy times as high as the moon;
What she did there I could not but ask it,
For in her hand she carried a broom.
"Old woman, old woman, old woman," said I,
"Whither oh whither oh whither so high?"
"To sweep the cobwebs from the sky,
And I shall be back again by and by."

OLD BETTY BLUE

Old Betty Blue
  Lost a holiday shoe,
What can old Betty do?
  Give her another
  To match the other,
And then she may swagger in two.

OLD MOTHER GOOSE

Old Mother Goose, when
She wanted to wander,
Would ride through the air
On a very fine gander.

OLD MOTHER HUBBARD

Old Mother Hubbard
  Went to the cupboard
  To get her poor dog a bone;
But when she came there
The cupboard was bare,
  And so the poor dog had none.

She went to the baker's
  To buy him some bread,
But when she came back
  The poor dog was dead.

She went to the joiner's
To buy him a coffin,
But when she came back
The poor dog was laughing.

She took a clean dish
To get him some tripe,
But when she came back
He was smoking his pipe.

She went to the fishmonger's
To buy him some fish,
And when she came back
He was licking the dish.

She went to the ale-house
To get him some beer,
But when she came back
The dog sat in a chair.

She went to the tavern
For white wine and red,
But when she came back
The dog stood on his head.

She went to the hatter's
To buy him a hat,
But when she came back
He was feeding the cat.

She went to the barber's
  To buy him a wig,
But when she came back
  He was dancing a jig.

She went to the fruiterer's
  To buy him some fruit,
But when she came back
  He was playing the flute.

She went to the tailor's
  To buy him a coat,
But when she came back
  He was riding a goat.

She went to the cobbler's
  To buy him some shoes,
But when she came back
  He was reading the news.

She went to the sempstress
To buy him some linen,
But when she came back
The dog was spinning.

She went to the hosier's
To buy him some hose,
But when she came back
He was dressed in his clothes.

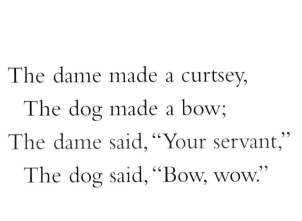

The dame made a curtsey,
The dog made a bow;
The dame said, "Your servant,"
The dog said, "Bow, wow."

173

ONE MISTY MOISTY MORNING

One misty moisty morning,
When cloudy was the weather,
There I met an old man
Clothed all in leather;

Clothed all in leather,
With cap under his chin—
How do you do, and how do you do,
And how do you do again!

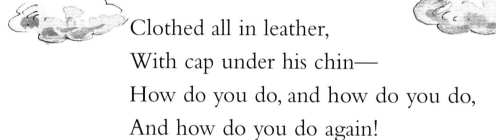

THERE WAS A CROOKED MAN

There was a crooked man, and he went a
  crooked mile,
He found a crooked sixpence against a
  crooked stile;
He bought a crooked cat, which caught a
  crooked mouse,
And they all lived together in a little crooked house.

AS I WALKED BY MYSELF

As I walked by myself,
And talked to myself,
  Myself said unto me,
Look to thyself,
Take care of thyself,
  For nobody cares for thee.

I answered myself,
And said to myself,
  In the self-same repartee,
Look to thyself,
Or not look to thyself,
  The self-same thing will be.

CROSS PATCH

Cross patch,
Draw the latch,
Sit by the fire and spin;
Take a cup,
And drink it up,
Then call your neighbours in.

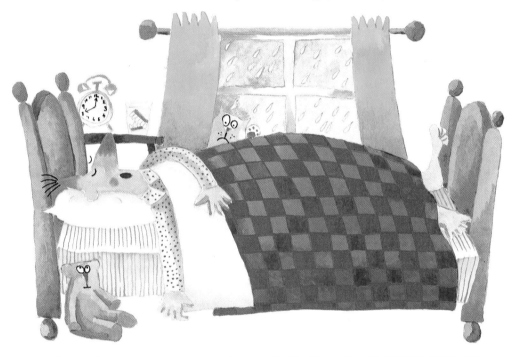

IT'S RAINING, IT'S POURING

It's raining, it's pouring,
The old man is snoring;
He went to bed and bumped his head
And couldn't get up in the morning.

WHEN I WAS A BACHELOR

When I was a bachelor I lived by myself,
And all the meat I got I put upon a shelf;
The rats and the mice did lead me such a life
That I went to London to get myself a wife.

The streets were so broad and the lanes were
   so narrow,
I could not get my wife home without a
   wheelbarrow;
The wheelbarrow broke, my wife got a fall,
Down tumbled wheelbarrow, little wife, and all.

JACK SPRAT

Jack Sprat could eat no fat,
His wife could eat no lean,
And so between the two of them
They licked the platter clean.

OLD JOE BROWN

Old Joe Brown, he had a wife,
  She was all of eight feet tall.
She slept with her head in the kitchen,
  And her feet stuck out in the hall.

JEREMIAH

Jeremiah
Jumped in the fire.
Fire was so hot
He jumped in the pot.
Pot was so little
He jumped in the kettle.
Kettle was so black
He jumped in the crack.
Crack was so high
He jumped in the sky.
Sky was so blue
He jumped in a canoe.
Canoe was so deep
He jumped in the creek.
Creek was so shallow
He jumped in the tallow.
Tallow was so soft
He jumped in the loft.
Loft was so rotten
He jumped in the cotton.
Cotton was so white
He jumped all night.

OLD JOHN MUDDLECOMBE

Old John Muddlecombe lost his cap,
He couldn't find it anywhere, the poor old chap.
He walked down the High Street, and everybody said,
"Silly John Muddlecombe, you've got it on your head!"

POOR OLD ROBINSON CRUSOE

Poor old Robinson Crusoe!
Poor old Robinson Crusoe!
  They made him a coat
  Of an old nanny goat,

  I wonder how they could do so!
With a ring a ting tang,
And a ring a ting tang,
  Poor old Robinson Crusoe!

RUB-A-DUB DUB

Rub-a-dub dub,
Three men in a tub,
And who do you think they be?
The butcher, the baker,
The candle-stick maker,
And they all jumped out of a rotten potato.

DOCTOR FOSTER WENT TO GLOUCESTER

Doctor Foster went to Gloucester,
  In a shower of rain;
He stepped in a puddle, up to his middle,
  And never went there again.

SOLOMON GRUNDY

Solomon Grundy,
Born on Monday,
Christened on Tuesday,
Married on
Wednesday,
Sick on Thursday,
Worse on Friday,
Died on Saturday,
Buried on Sunday,
That was the end
Of Solomon Grundy.

OLD KING COLE

Old King Cole
Was a merry old soul,
And a merry old soul was he;
He called for his pipe,
And he called for his bowl,
And he called for his fiddlers three.
Every fiddler had a fine fiddle,
And a very fine fiddle had he;
Twee tweedle dee, tweedle dee, went the fiddlers,
   Very merry men are we;
   Oh there's none so rare
   As can compare
With King Cole and his fiddlers three.

UNCLE JOHN IS VERY SICK

Uncle John is very sick, what shall we send him?

A piece of pie, a piece of cake, a piece of apple dumpling.

What shall we send it in? In a piece of paper.

Paper is not fine enough; in a golden saucer.

Who shall we send it by? By the governor's daughter.

Take her by the lily-white hand, and lead her over the water.

AT THE SIEGE OF BELLE-ISLE

At the siege of Belle-isle
I was there all the while,
All the while, all the while,
At the siege of Belle-isle.

THE GRAND OLD DUKE
OF YORK

The grand old Duke of York,
   He had ten thousand men;
He marched them up to the top of the hill,
   And he marched them down again!
And when they were up they were up,
   And when they were down they were down;
And when they were only halfway up,
   They were neither up nor down.

THERE WAS A KING, AND HE HAD THREE DAUGHTERS

There was a king, and he had three daughters,
And they all lived in a basin of water;
  The basin bended,
  My story's ended.
If the basin had been stronger,
My story would have been longer.

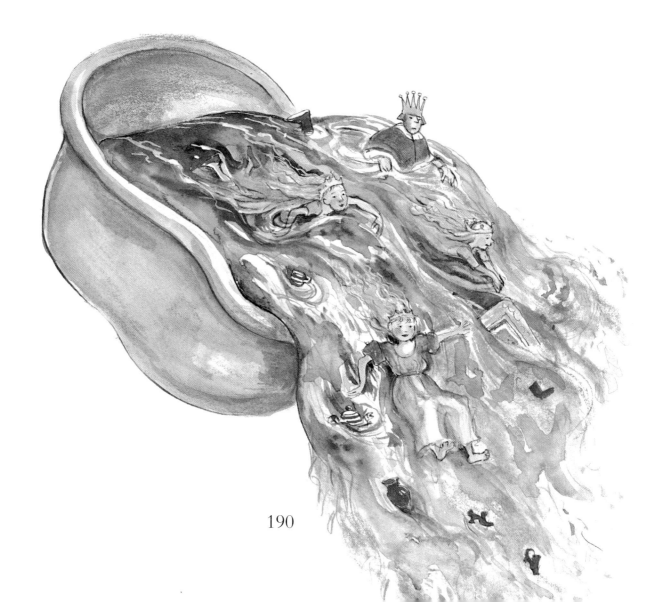

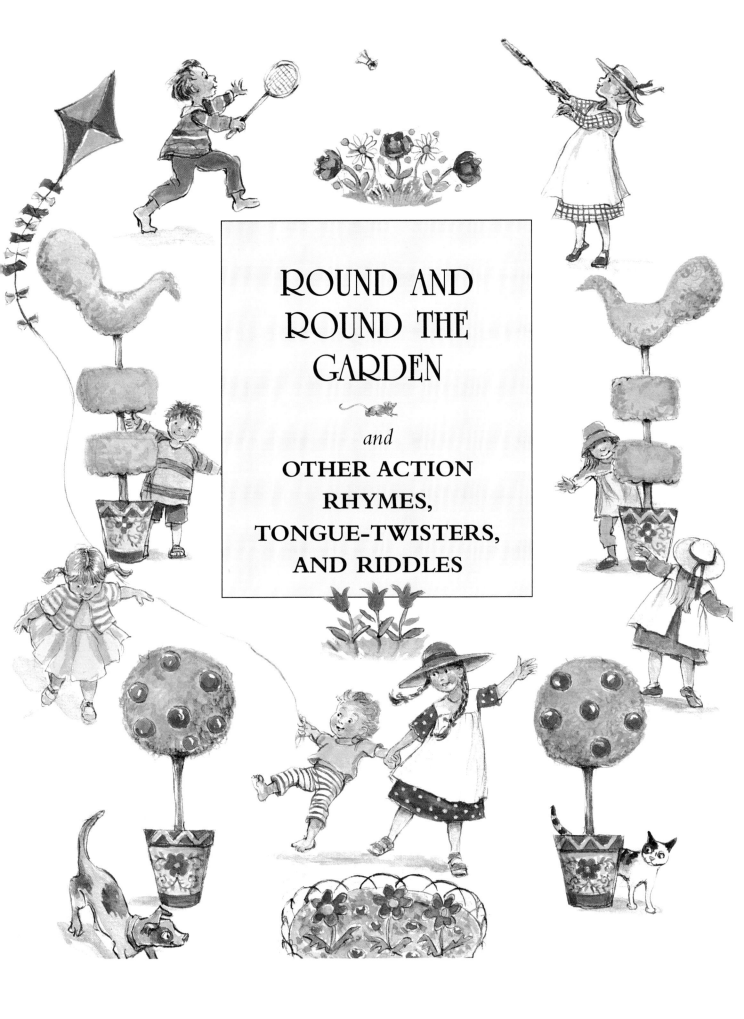

ROUND AND ROUND THE GARDEN

and

OTHER ACTION RHYMES, TONGUE-TWISTERS, AND RIDDLES

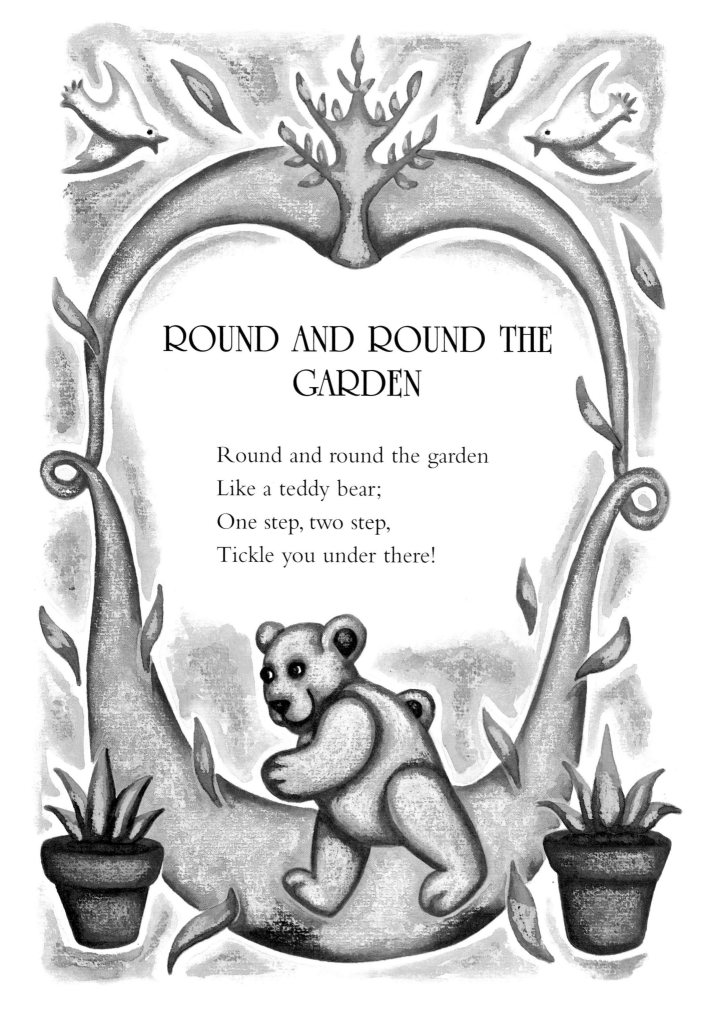

ROUND AND ROUND THE GARDEN

Round and round the garden
Like a teddy bear;
One step, two step,
Tickle you under there!

THIS LITTLE PIGGY

This little piggy went to market,
This little piggy stayed at home,
This little piggy had roast beef,
This little piggy had none,
And this little piggy cried, *Wee-wee-wee-wee-wee,*
　All the way home.

MY MOTHER AND YOUR MOTHER

My mother and your mother
  Went over the way;
Said my mother to your mother,
  It's chop-a-nose day!

A FACE GAME

Here sits the Lord Mayor;	*Forehead*
Here sit his two men;	*Eyes*
Here sits the cock;	*Right cheek*
Here sits the hen;	*Left cheek*
Here sit the little chickens;	*Tip of nose*
Here they run in,	*Mouth*
Chinchopper, chinchopper,	
Chinchopper, chin!	*Chuck the chin*

WASH, HANDS, WASH

Wash, hands, wash,
   Daddy's gone to plough;
If you want your hands washed,
   Have them washed now.

CLAP HANDS

Clap hands for Daddy coming
Down the wagon way,
With a pocketful of money
And a cartload of hay.

197

TO MARKET, TO MARKET

To market, to market,
  To buy a plum bun;
Home again, come again,
  Market is done.

TO MARKET, TO MARKET, TO BUY
A FAT PIG

To market, to market, to buy a fat pig,
  Home again, home again, dancing a jig;
Ride to the market to buy a fat hog,
  Home again, home again, jiggety-jog.

HOG
FOR SALE

THIS IS THE WAY THE LADIES RIDE

This is the way the ladies ride:
  Tri, tre, tre, tree,
  Tri, tre, tre, tree!
This is the way the ladies ride:
  Tri, tre, tre, tre, tri-tre-tre-tree!

This is the way the gentlemen ride:
  Gallop-a-trot,
  Gallop-a-trot!
This is the way the gentlemen ride:
  Gallop-a-gallop-a-trot!

This is the way the farmers ride:
  Hobbledy-hoy,
  Hobbledy-hoy!
This is the way the farmers ride:
  Hobbledy hobbledy-hoy!

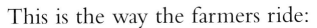

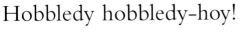

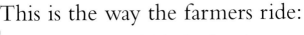

LEG OVER LEG

Leg over leg,
    As the dog went to Dover;
When he came to a stile,
    Jump he went over.

MICHAEL FINNEGAN

There was an old man called Michael Finnegan
He grew whiskers on his chinnegan
The wind came out and blew them in again
Poor old Michael Finnegan. *Begin again...*

RIDE A COCK-HORSE

Ride a cock-horse to Banbury Cross,
To see a fine lady ride on a white horse,
Rings on her fingers and bells on her toes,
She shall have music wherever she goes.

I AM A GOLD LOCK

FOR TWO VOICES

I am a gold lock.
I am a gold key.
I am a silver lock.
I am a silver key.
I am a brass lock.
I am a brass key.
I am a lead lock.
I am a lead key.
I am a monk lock.
I am a monk key!

I WENT UP ONE PAIR OF STAIRS

FOR TWO VOICES

I went up one pair of stairs.
Just like me.
I went up two pair of stairs.
Just like me.
I went into a room.
Just like me.
I looked out of a window.
Just like me.
And there I saw a monkey.
Just like me.

THE DARK WOOD

In the dark, dark wood, there was
  a dark, dark house,
And in that dark, dark house, there was
  a dark, dark room,
And in that dark, dark room, there was
  a dark, dark cupboard,
And in that dark, dark cupboard, there was
  a dark, dark shelf,
And on that dark, dark shelf, there was
  a dark, dark box,
And in that dark, dark box, there was a
  GHOST!

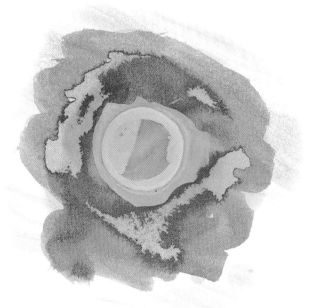

I MET A MAN

As I was going up the stair
I met a man who wasn't there.
He wasn't there again today—
Oh! how I wish he'd go away!

205

ADAM AND EVE AND PINCHME

Adam and Eve and Pinchme
Went down to the river to bathe.
Adam and Eve were drowned—
Who do you think was saved?

ME, MYSELF, AND I

Me, myself, and I—
We went to the kitchen and ate a pie.
Then my mother she came in
And chased us out with a rolling pin.

PETER PIPER

Peter Piper picked a peck of pickled pepper;
A peck of pickled pepper Peter Piper picked;
If Peter Piper picked a peck of pickled pepper,
Where's the peck of pickled pepper Peter Piper picked?

THE SHORTEST TONGUE-TWISTER

Peggy Babcock

MY GRANDMOTHER SENT ME

My grandmother sent me a new-fashioned three cornered cambric country cut handkerchief. Not an old-fashioned three cornered cambric country cut handkerchief, but a new-fashioned three cornered cambric country cut handkerchief.

ROBERT ROWLEY

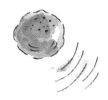

Robert Rowley rolled a round roll round,
A round roll Robert Rowley rolled round;
Where rolled the round roll Robert Rowley
    rolled round?

SWAN SWAM OVER THE SEA

Swan swam over the sea—
Swim, swan, swim,
Swan swam back again,
Well swum swan.

HEY, DOROLOT, DOROLOT!

Hey, dorolot, dorolot!
Hey, dorolay, dorolay!
Hey, my bonny boat, bonny boat,
Hey, drag away, drag away!

THERE WAS A MAN AND HIS NAME WAS DOB

There was a man, and his name was Dob,
And he had a wife, and her name was Mob,
And he had a dog, and he called it Cob,
And she had a cat, called Chitterabob.
 Cob, says Dob,
 Chitterabob, says Mob,
 Cob was Dob's dog,
 Chitterabob Mob's cat.

DIBBITY, DIBBITY, DIBBITY, DOE

Dibbity, dibbity, dibbity, doe,
Give me a pancake
  And I'll go.
Dibbity, dibbity, dibbity, ditter,
Please to give me
  A bit of a fritter.

ONE, TWO, THREE, FOUR, FIVE

One, two, three, four, five,
  I caught a fish alive;
Six, seven, eight, nine, ten,
  I let him go again.
Why did you let him go?
  Because he bit my finger so.

JACK BE NIMBLE

Jack be nimble,
And Jack be quick:
And Jack jump over
The candlestick.

TEDDY BEAR, TEDDY BEAR

Teddy bear, teddy bear,
Turn around.
Teddy bear, teddy bear,
Touch the ground.
Teddy bear, teddy bear,
Show your shoe.
Teddy bear, teddy bear,
That will do.

Teddy bear, teddy bear,
Go upstairs.
Teddy bear, teddy bear,
Say your prayers.
Teddy bear, teddy bear,
Turn out the light.
Teddy bear, teddy bear,
Say good night.

DANCE, LITTLE BABY

Dance, little baby, dance up high,
Never mind, baby, mother is by;
Crow and caper, caper and crow;
There, little baby, there you go;
Up to the ceiling, down to the ground,
Backwards and forwards, round and round;
Dance, little baby, and mother will sing,
With the merry coral, ding, ding, ding!

DANCE TO YOUR DADDY

Dance to your daddy,
My little babby;
Dance to your daddy,
My little lamb.

You shall have a fishy,
In a little dishy;
You shall have a fishy
When the boat comes in.

A THORN

I went to the wood and got it;
I sat me down and looked at it;
The more I looked at it the less I liked it;
And I brought it home because I couldn't help it.

TEETH

Thirty white horses upon a red hill,
Now they tramp, now they champ,
now they stand still.

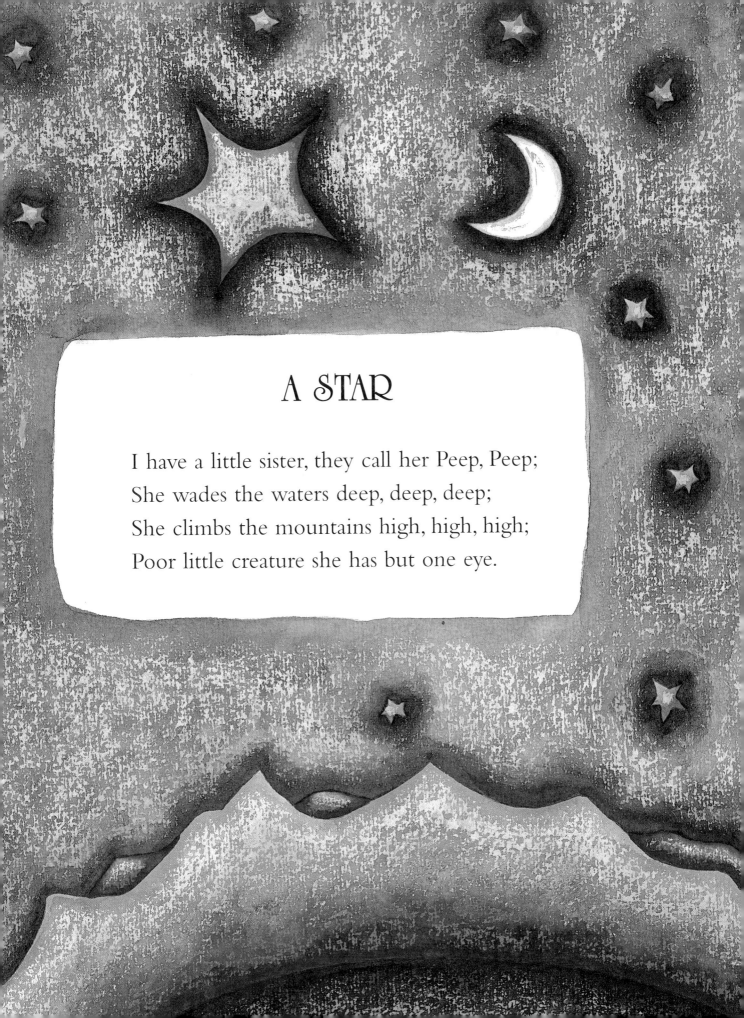

A STAR

I have a little sister, they call her Peep, Peep;
She wades the waters deep, deep, deep;
She climbs the mountains high, high, high;
Poor little creature she has but one eye.

A CANDLE

Little Nancy Etticoat
In a white petticoat,
And a red rose.
The longer she stands
The shorter she grows.

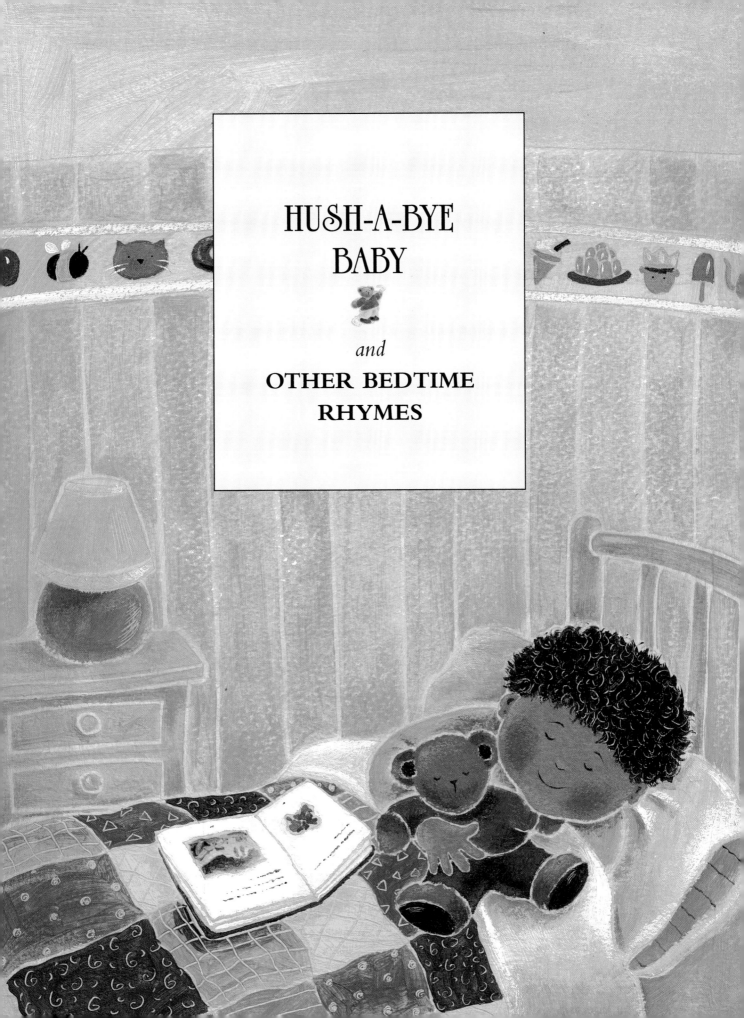

HUSH-A-BYE BABY

and

OTHER BEDTIME RHYMES

HUSH-A-BYE, BABY

Hush-a-bye, baby, on the tree top,
When the wind blows the cradle will rock;
When the bough breaks the cradle will fall,
Down will come baby, cradle and all.

ALL THE PRETTY
LITTLE HORSES

Hush-a-bye, don't you cry,
Go to sleepy little baby.
When you wake
You shall have
All the pretty little horses.
Blacks and bays,
Dapples and greys,
Coach and six white horses.

Hush-a-bye, don't you cry,
Go to sleepy little baby.
When you wake
You shall have cake
And all the pretty little horses.

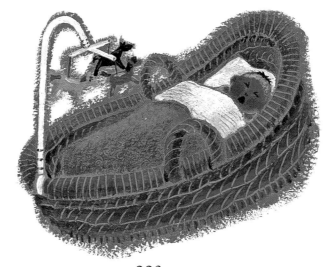

ROCK-A-BYE, BABY

Rock-a-bye, baby, thy cradle is green;
Father's a nobleman, Mother's a queen,
And Betty's a lady, and wears a gold ring,
And Johnny's a drummer, and drums for the King.

224

BYE, BABY BUNTING

Bye, baby bunting,
Father's gone a-hunting,
To fetch a little rabbit-skin
To wrap his baby bunting in.

COME TO BED, SAYS SLEEPY-HEAD

Come to bed,
Says Sleepy-head;
    "Tarry a while," says Slow;
"Put on the pot,"
Says Greedy-gut,
    "Let's sup before we go."

226

DIDDLE, DIDDLE, DUMPLING

Diddle, diddle, dumpling, my son John
Went to bed with his trousers on;
One shoe off, the other shoe on,
Diddle, diddle, dumpling, my son John.

GO TO BED, TOM

Go to bed, Tom,
Go to bed, Tom,
Tired or not, Tom,
Go to bed, Tom.

HIGGLEDY PIGGLEDY

Higgledy piggledy,
Here we lie,
Picked and plucked,
And put in a pie!

WEE WILLIE WINKIE

Wee Willie Winkie runs through the town,
Up-stairs and down-stairs in his nightgown,
Peeping through the keyhole, crying through the lock,
"Are the children in their beds, it's past eight o'clock?"

THE OLD WOMAN AND HER PIG

An old woman was sweeping her house, and she found
a little crooked sixpence. "What," said she, "shall I do
with this little sixpence? I will go to market, and buy a
little pig."

As she was coming home, she came to a stile; but the
pig would not go over the stile.

She went a little farther, and she met a dog. So she
said to the dog—

"Dog, dog, bite pig!

Pig won't get over the stile;

And I shan't get home tonight."

But the dog would not.

She went a little farther, and she met a stick.

So she said—

"Stick, stick, beat dog!

Dog won't bite pig?

Pig won't get over the stile,

And I shan't get home tonight."

But the stick would not.

She went a little farther, and she met a fire.

So she said—

"Fire, fire, burn stick!
Stick won't beat dog;
Dog won't bite pig;
Pig won't get over the stile,
And I shan't get home tonight."

But the fire would not.
She went a little farther, and she met water.
So she said—
"Water, water, quench fire!
Fire won't burn stick;
Stick won't beat dog;
Dog won't bite pig;
Pig won't get over the stile,
And I shan't get home tonight."

But the water would not.

She went a little farther, and she met an ox.

So she said—

"Ox, ox, drink water!

Water won't quench fire;

Fire won't burn stick;

Stick won't beat dog;

Dog won't bite pig;

Pig won't get over the stile,
And I shan't get home tonight."

But the ox would not.
She went a little farther, and she met a butcher.
So she said—
"Butcher, butcher, kill ox!
Ox won't drink water;
Water won't quench fire;
Fire won't burn stick;
Stick won't beat dog;
Dog won't bite pig;
Pig won't get over the stile,
And I shan't get home tonight."

But the butcher would not.
She went a little farther, and she met a rope.
So she said—
"Rope, rope, hang butcher!
Butcher won't kill ox;
Ox won't drink water;
Water won't quench fire;
Fire won't burn stick;

Stick won't beat dog;
Dog won't bite pig;
Pig won't get over the stile,
And I shan't get home tonight."

But the rope would not.
She went a little farther, and she met a rat.
So she said—
"Rat, rat, gnaw rope!
Rope won't hang butcher;
Butcher won't kill ox;
Ox won't drink water;
Water won't quench fire;
Fire won't burn stick;
Stick won't beat dog;
Dog won't bite pig;
Pig won't get over the stile,
And I shan't get home tonight."

But the rat would not.
She went a little farther, and she met a cat.
So she said—

"Cat, cat, kill rat;
Rat won't gnaw rope;
Rope won't hang butcher;
Butcher won't kill ox;
Ox won't drink water;
Water won't quench fire;
Fire won't burn stick;
Stick won't beat dog;
Dog won't bite pig;
Pig won't get over the stile,
And I shan't get home tonight."

The cat said, "If you will give me a saucer of milk, I will kill the rat."

So the old woman gave the cat the milk, and when she had lapped up the milk—

The cat began to kill the rat;
The rat began to gnaw the rope;
The rope began to hang the butcher;
The butcher began to kill the ox;
The ox began to drink the water;
The water began to quench the fire;
The fire began to burn the stick;
The stick began to beat the dog;
The dog began to bite the pig;
The pig jumped over the stile,
And so the old woman got home that night.

THREE WISE MEN OF GOTHAM

Three wise men of Gotham
Went to sea in a bowl:
And if the bowl had been stronger,
My song would have been longer.

JACKANORY

I'll tell you a story
Of Jackanory,
And now my story's begun;
I'll tell you another
Of Jack his brother,
And now my story's done.

239

THE KEY OF THE KINGDOM

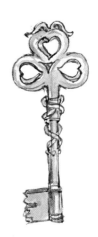

This is the key of the kingdom:
In that kingdom is a city,
In that city is a town,
In that town there is a street,
In that street there was a lane,
In that lane there is a yard,
In that yard there is a house,
In that house there waits a room,
In that room there is a bed,
On that bed there is a basket,
  A basket of flowers.

Flowers in the basket,
Basket on the bed,
Bed in the chamber,
Chamber in the house,
House in the weedy yard,
Yard in the winding lane,
Lane in the broad street,
Street in the high town,
Town in the city,
City in the kingdom:
    This is the key of the kingdom.
    Of the kingdom this is the key.

I HAD A LITTLE NUT TREE

I had a little nut tree, nothing would it bear,
But a silver nutmeg, and a golden pear;
The King of Spain's daughter came to visit me,
And all for the sake of my little nut tree.
I skipped over water, I danced over sea,
And all the birds of the air couldn't catch me.

HOW MANY MILES TO BABYLON?

How many miles to Babylon?—
Threescore and ten.
Can I get there by candlelight?—
Aye, and back again!

TOMMY TROT

Tommy Trot, a man of law,
Sold his bed and lay upon straw:
Sold the straw and slept on grass,
To buy his wife a looking-glass.

TUMBLING

In jumping and tumbling
   We spend the whole day,
Till night by arriving
   Has finished our play.

What then? One and all,
   There's no more to be said,
As we tumbled all day,
   So we tumble to bed.

MATTHEW, MARK, LUKE, AND JOHN

Matthew, Mark, Luke, and John
Bless the bed that I lie on.
Before I lay me down to sleep,
I pray the Lord my soul to keep.

Four corners to my bed,
Four angels there are spread;
Two at the foot, two at the head:
Four to carry me when I'm dead.

I go by sea, I go by land:
The Lord made me with His right hand.
Should any danger come to me,
Sweet Jesus Christ deliver me.

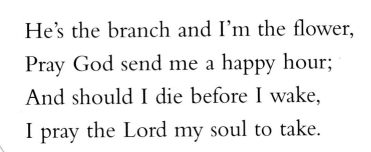

He's the branch and I'm the flower,
Pray God send me a happy hour;
And should I die before I wake,
I pray the Lord my soul to take.

FOR EVERY EVIL UNDER THE SUN

For every evil under the sun,
There is a remedy, or there is none.
If there be one, try and find it;
If there be none, never mind it.

SALLY GO ROUND THE MOON

Sally go round the moon,
Sally go round the stars;
Sally go round the moon
On a Sunday afternoon.

STAR LIGHT, STAR BRIGHT

Star light, star bright,
First star I see tonight,
I wish I may, I wish I might,
Have the wish I wish tonight.

I SEE THE MOON

I see the moon,
   And the moon sees me;
God bless the moon,
   And God bless me.

INDEX OF FIRST LINES

Be bow bend it,
My book's ended.
If you don't like it,
You may mend it.